How to be a Successful
Politician

How to be a Successful Politician

The Ultimate Guide for New and Seasoned Politicos

BRIAN C. HAGGERTY

BCH Enterprise, LLC
c/o Brian C. Haggerty
645 Second Avenue
Lyndhurst, NJ 07071

www.BrianHaggerty.com

ISBN-13: 9780692955505
ISBN-10: 069295550X

Dedicated to my two great-grandfathers, Charles Carella and John E. Guidetti, and my grandfather, Nicholas A. Carella, whose legacies, both politically and personally, inspired and helped to make me who and what I am.

Contents

Introduction

AS THE OLD adage goes, "It's not what you know, it's who you know". Such is the great game of politics. It is the business of relationships, alliances, influence and power; filled with intrigue and played like chess. To get anywhere in politics, whether you are seeking office or looking to be a player, you need friends. A good political mind will seek to find common ground among others. He or she can see the larger picture and recognize the importance in building bridges, rather than burning them. If you truly want to be a successful politician—regardless of the role you choose to play—you must understand that everyone has their own agenda. For most, it is the issues about which they are most passionate. For others, it could be strictly business. In politics, the fastest route between two points is a straight line. Therefore, being open to what others are seeking is vital. A keen political mind will work toward his or her goal while helping others achieve theirs and avoiding meaningless drama and needless battles.

Regardless of your political leanings, it is best to make friends with people on all sides of a political issue. As the

Rolling Stones song says, you can't always get what you want. But, you can get a great deal more than others if you play the game by the rules. Those who last the longest and are the most successful in this business are those who understand that to get, you must give. You must build consensus. One cannot expect to be on the winning side every time. Nor can you expect to always be on the receiving end. Politics is give and take.

By being someone who is amicable and open-minded, and has developed that reputation, you can expect to be in a good position most times; even when you or your people are not in office. In essence, this is what is referred to as the establishment. The Political Establishment is not limited to Washington. There is an establishment at each level; state, county and local. Members of the establishment generally maintain influence. They do so because of the relationships and reputation they developed over a period of time. Whenever you see anyone who has survived a long time in politics, regardless of which party or power-base holds office, it is because they have developed good relationships with people within all areas of the political spectrum.

Despite all of this, politics, and politicians, especially, are not always held to such high regard by the public. The sheer word carries with itself a great many negative connotations. Every day there are stories popping up somewhere regarding political corruption or some politician, somewhere, engaging in something unbecoming a public official. In my opening sentence above, I said that "It's not what you know, it's who you know". To the extent that to be successful you need relationships is true. However, you still need to know what to do. You must have some sense of public trust and a commitment to the greater good.

Politicians are human beings. As such, they are flawed. But it is we who have the ability to take control of, and care for, our image. While I attempt to describe much of the behaviors of successful politicians, I do so with the caveat that to be effective leaders and to have good government that works effectively, we need more and more good politicians. The personal skills in this book will certainly help you become successful. But only you, the politician, can make the individual choice to be the best that you can be and model yourself with distinction, class, and to be the role model you should. In other words, you can have lots of style, but you also need the substance if you are to fulfill the public's idea of what and who their elected officials should actually be.

Four years ago, I decided to step away from holding elected office to focus upon my career. And while I may have left politics as an office holder, politics in no way has left me. It's in my DNA. My family's political roots date back over 130 years to my great-great grandfather in New York City and spans each generation to now include a multitude of cousins and other relatives, all of whom dwell in the political world from a local to a national level. As a result, I always see things through a political lens. I understand the rules of the game and have the benefit of those 130 years on so many levels.

*"All the worlds a stage; and all of the men and
women merely players"*

WM. SHAKESPEARE

Of course, I come from the state of New Jersey. As such, my experience and point of view are shaped accordingly. I also focus much of the book on local politics, as there are far more local politicians than any other. Hence, this is what the legendary Speaker of the House, Tip O'Neill, meant when he said that "All politics is local". The majority of politicians, regardless of how high of an office they may hold, most likely got started locally. Locally, to me, is any position within a township or county.

To put this in a numerical perspective, there are 537 federal elected offices (Which includes the President, Vice President, members of the House and Senate). However, there are well over 500,000 elected offices in the country. This book for those 500,000.

Politics is also theater. It is a combination of image and perception. While I find myself behind the scenes teaching these tactics and skills to executives, business people and other politicos, it is the experiences I have had which can apply to any position of power and influence. This book is designed to offer simple advice, pointers and descriptions for anyone who is seeking to run for office, holds office, gets involved in politics or is just curious. These are universal principles which can help you become successful in this business. I have seen people come and go like a revolving door. But the truly successful politicos are those who play smart and focus on the long-game; the ones who possess great style, substance and character.

I intentionally do not discuss campaigning in this book. Rather, this book is solely intended to teach someone how to be a better, more successful politician with the hope of instilling the importance of character. If the portrayal of politicians is going to improve, it can only do so when politicians practice good politics. That is the foundation of good government.

When my friend, and long-time political mentor, Louis J. Stellato, Chairman of the Democratic Party of Bergen County, NJ, invited me to present to elected officials on these topics, I knew it was time to write this book. I hope this will give the reader an eye-opener into the wonderful world of politics and that of those who play the game; the politicians. These principles work and can work for you if you are willing to learn them, incorporate them into your life and adhere to them always.

1

Having Good People Skills

A SUCCESSFUL POLITICIAN MUST have good people skills. I would say make that superb people skills, in fact. Every single person you meet is a prospective vote, volunteer, supporter, center of influence, fundraiser, etc. And each of those prospective people will all talk to other people who will talk to other people and so on, and so on. Just like the old Faberge Organic Shampoo commercial from years back. If you have refined your people skills to such a degree that you possess strong likeability, then your popularity, reputation and circle of friends will grow exponentially. If you do not, then you won't. Plain and simple.

Even if you have an ego of immense proportions, I would hope that you have the intellect to understand how to temper that ego and use your people skills to cause others to want to follow you and remain loyal. Politics is about people. The more people like you, the better your reputation, the farther others will propel you in the political arena. Therefore, no discussion of how to be a good politician would be complete without a 101 level course on how to develop good people skills which will serve you well in your political life.

SELF-AWARENESS

Self-awareness is a recurring theme you will read throughout this book. It is the foundation for self-improvement. Without it, you would not be aware of the areas in which you need improvement; whether it is with public speaking, how you dress, how you carry yourself and the over-all image you convey. It also extends to our character and what habits we possess; good and bad. Without a doubt, every successful politician I have ever known is highly self-aware. In fact, high self-awareness is what defines celebrities, rock stars and national politicians. They are all highly self-aware and have worked at self-improvement and refinement for many years.

Almost anyone can develop effective people and social skills. All it takes is the desire and the practice. The reason it takes practice is because, like any skill, you are basically creating a habit through a new, learned and repeated behavior. The more you repeat the behavior, the more it becomes a habit and the less you will need to think about it consciously.

The best way to start yourself off is to do a complete evaluation of yourself. For this, I recommend either retaining a coach or at least someone who has the experience in dealing with people and communication skills. You can also watch yourself on video to critique yourself. But, understand that you need to accept the constructive criticism of your coach or professional who will point out the various areas in which you can make improvements. Here is an exercise I use in my teachings which will help anyone truly get a better idea of the differences between how they view themselves and how they are viewed by others. It is often quite an eye-opener for many.

EXERCISE TO DEVELOP SELF-AWARENESS

Get a blank sheet of paper and write out a list of words that you would use to describe yourself. Don't just flatter yourself. Be critical. Write it all down; the good, the bad and even the ugly. If you are someone who is habitually late, write that down. If you have a lack of patience, write that down, too.

Now, after you've completed your list, I want you to go to the people closest to you; family, friends, business associates with whom you are close, etc. Ask them to write down a list of words that they would use to describe you. But here's the thing, you must explain to them that you are engaging in an exercise of self-awareness and that you need and expect them to be blatantly honest. This is important or the exercise will not work. This is why a successful politician needs to learn how to accept constructive criticism. If you are not open to your personal flaws (And we all have them), you will only hear what you want to hear. You will wind up living in a political bubble, will lose touch with yourself and others and will not last long in the game.

You do not need to share with anyone else what you wrote or what others wrote about you. This is purely an exercise for you. As you read what others write and their perceptions about you, you may be very surprised to see some things you never would have expected. This is what you want! This is how you develop self-awareness and begin the process of refinement. Self-reflect on what you do, what you say and the interactions you had, daily. Keep these pages in a safe place. You will want to refer to them often. You will also want to go back to those trusted people in your life from time to time and ask them to repeat the exercise. When their feedback begins to show improvement upon your personal flaws, you are performing the exercise perfectly.

I will speak in a later chapter about the need for self-reflection and mindfulness and how such practice will help us to recognize and change our behaviors accordingly. But most important is to spend some time, daily, in reflection of the results of the exercise and to ask oneself daily if we are making the conscious effort to evolve into a better, more refined professional and one who represents him or herself with dignity, class and distinction.

INTRODUCING YOURSELF AND HAVING A CONVERSATION

Every relationship, friendship and association begins when two people meet each other and introduce themselves. This is the point-zero of politics; the golden first impression which forms the basis of all relationships. This is something that is not taught in schools. Generally, people learn to do this well by either watching, having a role model, a personal coach or trial and error. Most of the public are not always aware of the subtleties and nuances of introductions. Here are the main points to learn and practice in step format:

- Have good posture, stand tall, smile and look people directly in the eye.
- Do not have a Smartphone in your hand or you'll be tempted to look at it rather than the person you are meeting.
- Walk up to someone and extend your right hand; stepping into the handshake with your right foot forward.
- As you are doing so, look right into their eyes and introduce yourself. Mention your first and last name and do so clearly and loudly enough that they can hear you.
- Your handshake should be firm, not weak. But also, do not squeeze someone's hand.
- The handshake should be equal. Make sure your hand is perpendicular to the floor. Do not face your palm down or up.
- Once you have fully clasped one another's hand, move your hand up and down within a few inches for four or five shakes and let go.
- As the other person repeats his or her name, make sure you repeat their name. In fact, most forget a person's name seconds after hearing it because they are so focused on everything else about you that this slips through their mind.

- Make some sort of mental connection regarding their name and be ready to repeat it throughout the conversation.
- Make sure you have established personal space. Few people are aware of personal space. If you are in their space, they will not tell you, they will show you by backing up. Be aware of this and never step toward someone who has backed away. Stay at arm's length.
- Be sure that your body is facing the person. This includes your feet. They should point toward the other person. Refrain from putting your hands in your pockets and keep them visible.
- Begin a conversation by asking simple questions of the other person such as where they are from, what do they do for a living, etc.
- Seek to find something in common by asking questions.
- NEVER, repeat, never monopolize the conversation. This is biggest mistake most make.
- ALWAYS show more interest in who they are and what they do. They may very well monopolize the conversation due to a lack of awareness, but your job is to pretend you love every bit of it.
- Whenever the times comes when you need to end the conversation, just say something like this: *"Well, I don't want to take up any more of your time. But it has been such a pleasure to meet you! I look forward to speaking with you again."*

The previous steps are quite academic. But there are a great many things going on in the background and under the surface. Granted, as a politician, you will need to engage in hundreds of conversations which you otherwise would not. Not all of them will be exciting or enriching. But, unlike an ordinary person who can walk away at will, you must be polite. You must learn how to be a good listener. In fact, listening, as we will discuss later, is the most important communication skill there is. If you are not listening, you will not know what someone wants nor what to say. Many hear, not so many listen.

Think about you own life and those whom you have met and have instantly liked. What is it that would make someone so attractive to people upon their meeting? You will find they mostly possess the same things; a smile, likeability, great energy and the ability to make you feel valued and important. These are all things that anyone, with focus and work, can learn and integrate into their personality.

The entire concept of the handshake and introduction is to make a great impression. Ultimately, by coming across as approachable, friendly and interested in the other person's life or viewpoint; and being aware of things such as personal space, you are leaving that person with a lasting, good impression of you. When I roleplay these instances with clients and students, I always ask the same question, *"Are you more or less likely to want to be in the company of someone who makes you feel safe, secure and good about yourself?"* The answer is obvious. This is what you are aiming for. Remember, you are the public persona. It is you who should be polished enough to know how to handle all people in all situations; good, bad or boring. Yes, it can be boring at times. But, to quote Hyman Roth from the Godfather Part 2, "*This is the business we've chosen*".

KEEP TRACK OF THE PEOPLE YOU MEET

It is a good idea to keep a written or computer journal, a log or some sort of record of the people you meet and the things about which you spoke. Personal things, such as family events, accomplishments or even sickness should be remembered so that when you encounter the person again, they will be very honored and amazed that you remembered something that was important to them. The more we demonstrate that people are valued, the better our relationships and the more effective those who govern can be.

MAKING EMOTIONAL CONNECTIONS

In the public speaking and speech chapter, I will explain more about emotional connections and the impact they have on an audience. But even when meeting someone you should always seek to find a point of connection with someone in some aspect of their life, their goals, dreams, aspirations, etc. Emotional connections can be far more lasting than anything else. In many cases, they can outweigh the intellect. This is why those who use divisive politics as a weapon will always make it about emotion rather than fact. Once you connect with someone on a deep emotional level, such as sharing important things in common, you deepen the relationship and give it a sense of value and importance that is beyond that of a mere acquaintance. As a politician, the more you know someone, the more human they become, the more likely you are to treat them as such.

BE REAL

Sadly, politicians are often regarded as fake, or feigning sincerity. Who knows, you may very well not have a single care for anyone in your body. I would hope that you do. However, as a politician, you have the ability to help reduce and eliminate that reputation by upholding the humanity of others and doing the right thing for them. If you act the role of humble servant, you will do a great deal to change the public's perception. I have found that in my experience, the majority of those in politics are genuinely real, good people. A few bad apples always upset the cart. And, the bad perceptions are mostly institutional and have been so for decades or longer. But the future can and should be defined by what we do now.

COMMENTARY

Your first impression is vital when forging new friendships and relationships. If you develop the awareness of how you make others feel, both in word and deed, you can build superior people skills which are absolutely necessary to become a successful politician. But, in addition to a good first impression, you also need to possess many traits. In the next chapter, we'll examine some of those traits in what I call the Top Ten Habits of Successful Politicians. In the meantime, remember these principles of politics:

- People are far more likely to vote for someone who makes them feel good.
- People are more likely to vote based upon emotion.
- People generally vote against people, rather than for them, which is why being likable is vital.
- People are far more likely to vote for someone who has asked for their support and makes them feel important.
- People are more likely to vote for someone they know versus someone they do not.
- Be the embodiment of all that is good and do your part to uphold a solid reputation among your peers.

2

The Top 10 Habits of Successful Politicians

WHILE BY NO means all inclusive, this is a list of ten principles which all successful politicians follow to one degree or another. In my experience and observations, those who adhere to these principles win the most, last the longest and maintain the greatest influence.

1. Always show up.

98% of politics is showing up. It's no different than life. If you want to be a successful politician, you need to make appearances. Lots of them. One of the secrets of politics is that people are far more likely to vote for someone they have met and with whom they've interacted. Even if you do not stay very long at an event, people will always appreciate the fact that you took the time out of your otherwise busy schedule to show up. (*A Big No-No: Never fail to acknowledge an invitation. If you are invited to something and receive an invitation via mail or e-mail, always make sure that you answer the invite. This is an area in which politicians are extremely neglectful. If you are unable to attend, be sure to write or call the person and thank them for the invitation. The sheer act of acknowledging someone's invitation and showing respect to them will go a long way in politics. And, it will most certainly NOT be forgotten. Be different from the rest; always respond. It's what you are supposed to do!*)

2. Always be accessible.

A successful politician is one who is highly accessible. If people know they can reach out to you, they will vote for you. This is also a skill. Some politicians are horrible about returning phone calls, e-mails, texts, etc.. Every mode of communication, no matter how insignificant, is important in order for you to establish and maintain a superior reputation of accessibility and reliability. Failing to return messages of any sort is a sign of disrespect. I know of many in the political world who never return phone calls and fail to acknowledge other's concerns. However, when these politicos need you, they expect you to call them back immediately. Being busy is no excuse. Everyone is busy. This requires discipline on your part to learn how to make better use of your time in order to return phone calls and other forms of correspondence. On the road to recovery of the unfortunate reputation politicians have, this is a huge step in our doing our job and earning the trust and respect of the public whom we serve.

One of the busiest and most important political persons I know always returns phone calls in a timely manner. With three phones on him at all times, Lou Stellato, the Democratic Chairman of Bergen County, NJ is one of the most accessible politicos I know. In the thirty-plus adult years I have known him, he always returns everyone's phone calls; usually within a few hours. This superior and successful habit is also what contributed to his great successes in his business and political life.

3. Never make a commitment unless you are certain you can keep it!

This is probably the biggest mistake everyone makes, not just politicians. After all, we have all been the victim of broken promises at some point by family, friends, companies, etc. For politicians, though, this seems to be among the biggest of faults in terms of their reputations. Politicians seem to be well-known for breaking their promises. Remember, politicians are just people. And, like people, they make mistakes. Ordinary people are constantly making promises and breaking them, so politicians did not invent this practice. But, for some reason, they seem to own it. This is why it is vital that we learn how to avoid our making empty promises.

When in the moment, human beings have a strong tendency to want to say things that will gain the approval of others. This is natural. In that moment, their intentions may be good. However, unless you stop, think and ask yourself the following questions before you commit, you are doing far more harm to yourself and your reputation—and the reputation of all politicos.

- Is this something I have the ability to do?
- Is this the right thing to do?
- What other factors are involved which may hinder my fulfilling this commitment/promise?
- Do I have the time, resources and know-how to fulfill this promise?
- Do I even want to do this?
- Do I have any other commitments which may be affected by the fulfillment of this promise?

Your answers to these questions will help you be able to gauge whether or not you should make that commitment. However, if unsure of any, the right approach is <u>not to make any commitment.</u> Never, I repeat, never make an empty promise to get someone's vote. You only wind up making that person angry and resentful toward you. While you may gain their vote under false pretenses, you will lose their vote and their support in the future once you failed to fulfill your commitment.

Always be honest. You can most certainly tell someone that you will do your very best to help them, but you will earn more of their respect if you say, *"I cannot promise you something about which I am not certain. And I would never want to commit to something until I am certain."* You will never fail with this approach. If you subsequently are able to fulfill your commitment, you will be seen as a hero to the person or persons.

However, if you commit and fail, the person or persons will lose respect for you. And once respect is lost, it is nearly impossible to regain. What's more, that person will talk to other people who will talk to other people, etc. Let's work together to change the reputation of our leaders. It starts with each of us, individually.

4. Always make everyone feel important.

It's easy to cuddle up to the big donors, but money alone will not get you elected. You must give attention to the voters. If you are the type of person who wants to run for office in order to bask in the light of self-importance, then understand something: you are already important by virtue of your position. As discussed in the previous chapter, your job is not to make yourself important. Your job is to make people feel important. Handing out Resolutions, cutting ribbons and otherwise answering letters, invitations and Christmas/holiday cards are all a part of touching the voters personally while acknowledging and maintaining their support. Again, keep notes on everyone with whom you come into contact. Find out their birthdays, important life events, sick or ill family members and always follow up with them by asking for updates. This will absolutely set you apart from others and will endear the people to you. *All successful politicians do just that.* That is why they are successful. It takes work, but all great things which lead to success take work. *A little anecdote to underscore this lesson: When I was 20 years old, I was at a small gathering of politicians who received candidates running for the state legislature. One of whom was running for the Assembly was coming up to each of us to shake hands. When this candidate got to me, instead of making eye-contact, he, instead, looked around to find someone more important. He shook my hand, but his eyes were looking for someone more important. In the end, I did not vote for this person because of this.*

5. Assume everything is on the record:

As a politician, always assume that every conversation, phone call and correspondence is on the record. If it is a phone call, assume it is being recorded. If it is an e-mail or letter, assume it can appear in print in a newspaper or in a political flyer. Today, everyone is equipped with a listening device built right into their phones. Anyone can record anything. Due to the sad distrust of politicians, members of the public often will record their conversations with politicians without their knowledge. While private conversations among private citizens have legal protections, politicians are public figures and therefore anything they say is subject to the Open Public Records Act or Sunshine Laws. This applies to your social media accounts (Please see the section on social media). As a politician, you are, sad to say, fair game for anything. Anything can and will be used against you. Be careful and always assume that what you say is on the record.

6. Never speak ill of anyone:

In politics, your political enemy of today could very well be your ally tomorrow. Remember, politics makes for strange bed fellows. And, as Don Corleone said to his hot-headed son,

Sonny, "*Never tell anyone outside of the family what you are thinking.*" It does a politician no good to bad mouth someone else. Believe me, it will get repeated and often will be repeated worse than what you may have said. Be mindful and weary, also, of those who badmouth others to you. They may be trying to get you to do likewise and then carry those words back to the other person. At best, they are showing you who they are. Keep all of your negative opinions about others to yourself.

If you wish to speak out strongly against an issue, by all means do so. But don't get personal in politics. It is a business. In my many years of campaigns; whether they were mine or someone else's, I have been on the same side with people, only to find myself on an opposing side in the next election. By never speaking ill of anyone, you will be assured that the merry-go-round of politics will bring those people back your way and on your side when the right time comes. I realize you may need to bite your tongue many times, but in the end, it is well worth it.

People absolutely LOVE to repeat what a politician said about someone else if it was not favorable. If it was favorable, they don't care. Instead, they love drama and crave self-importance by repeating the things they know will cause drama or dissention. Unless it is your long-time friend, spouse or family member, never assume you can trust anyone. It is a sad state of affairs, but it is the truth. You never know who it is you will need to align with politically in your next, or future campaigns. This goes a long, long way in your political life.

7. Beware of the free meal:

Some get into politics for the perks. Whether it is the restaurant owner who does not want to give you a bill, a contractor who offers to do work on your home for nothing or someone who offers some kind of arrangement to you, such as use of their oceanfront condo, you need to be very much aware and extremely careful and suspect.

Contrary to public belief, the overwhelming majority of politicians are not on the take. The old days of paper bags filled with cash payoffs are long gone and anyone engaging in such practice is an idiot. However, as human beings, the temptations are there and they are real. It can creep upon you without your even noticing. Many politicians will rationalize in their mind why it is ok to take someone up on a free offer. But the end result is the same. Once you accept, you are compromised. So, whether it is free tickets to a baseball game, use of their ocean front condominium, free or reduced rent on a property, having business steered your way because of your position or anything which even gives the appearance of impropriety, stay as far away from it as the East is from the West. It will tarnish your reputation and will bite you in the end.

Keeping yourself free from compromise is not easy. Sometimes, things seem so innocent until someone asks you for a favor which may involve illegal or unethical things. I would say more so unethical than illegal. However, if such a person showered you with gifts, advantages or anything for which others pay and you did not, you are now compromised. Again, by doing what is right, we uphold our positions of public trust and work together toward improving our collective reputations as politicians.

8. Pick your battles:

This is politics 101. To be effective in politics, you do not want to be the person who, every day, every month, every year, is fighting every battle he or she can find. If you do, you will not be taken seriously. Like the boy who cried wolf, people grow tired of anyone who is always on the rampage with one thing or another. Instead, pay very close attention to an issue. See who is involved, what is at stake and decide whether or not there is anything you can contribute or can capitalize upon that increases or advances your position. Timing is everything. To gain the most attention and to be the most effective, be sure to pick the right time to insert yourself into an issue. Make sure you fully assess the ramifications, both short and long-term, of your involvement. Once you take ownership of something, it is yours.

9. Avoid drama:

Nothing does more to knock you off balance than to get caught up in the drama of campaigns and politics in general. Most of the drama will unfold during a campaign. Every day, someone, somewhere, will want to tell you what so-and-so said, what so-and-so did or what such-and-such are doing. Unless it has tactical value, ignore it. Most of it is pure nonsense being bantered about by people who relish in drama. Without even realizing it, many people love drama. It is usually the sign of a mind which has little else to fill it. All drama can do is get you off-balance and off-message.

With social media and the emergence of the Internet, people's opinions are on parade. Social media offered a platform to people whose opinions never would have been heard. Sadly, most people's opinions are completely uninformed. As a result, and because they lack information and facts, they resort to ad hominen attacks. My advice to all politicos is to do your best to avoid reading these types of threads on Social Media during a campaign. All it will do is get under your skin, into your head and do exactly what your detractors want it to do; cause you to lose your mind and lose your focus. It is important to understand that nothing written anonymously on social media or some rouge message board will likely get you votes or cause you to lose them. Only insiders read them. Stay focused, stay vigilant and if something appears somewhere that does have merit, value or can be a possible problem, your campaign consultant will handle it. As for you, keep campaigning.

10. Never forget where you came from:

No matter who you are, nor how high the office to which you are elected, there will always be those who helped you get there. This is another part often over-looked by politicians. They sometimes forget who helped them. Don't let a false ego get in your way. Be sure to remember, acknowledge and thank the people who got you to where you are. I have witnessed politicos turn on many of those who actually helped them; falsely allowing their ego to assume it is they who won on their own. They generally wind up going to way of all turncoats; they lose.

It's nice to think we are special and that we got to where we are because we are brilliant and wonderful! Well, your mother will always feel that way. Perhaps your spouse and children, too. But the reality is that everyone got to where they are because of the help of others. If you forget those people, they will be sure to remind you one way or another!

Remember, where you come from is what helps to define your values, experience and every strong element of character which you bring to the table in your role as a politician. Humility will always rule the day. No one likes someone who has a large, overly-inflated opinion of themselves. Again, this is the image far too many have of politicians. Therefore, again, our duty is to uphold the right elements of character in order to strengthen our reputation as leaders.

COMMENTARY

As you continue to develop your self-awareness, always be examining every aspect of yourself. Do you practice all of the previous ten habits? If so, that is great! You either are or will certainly become a successful politician. If you adhere to most, that's also good because now you will be aware of the others. If you fail to follow a majority of these, you have work to do. Remember, even if you lose an election, that does not mean you should take that as a personal rejection. All politicians win and lose. The pendulum swings back and forth. If it has swung in the opposite direction, you can rest assured that it will swing back. As long as you are prepared when it comes back your way, you will win. If you uphold and demonstrate good character coupled with humility and likeability, you are doing your part in redefining the role of a politician.

3

The Types of People
Involved in Politics

ELECTED OFFICIALS ARE only a part of the political world. While the whole arena seems to revolve around the elected officials, it's the various people, voters, organizations, interests and groups which helped to put him or her in that elected position—as well as those who work against them— who comprise the political arena. While this list is by no means exhaustive, it describes the type of people whom one usually encounters in the business of politics. Some people may very well be a combination of two or more classifications. Best to understand each so that we can recognize any when they are encountered. While you may have or think of some others, this is merely from my own perspective and experience.

1. The Elected Official.

Politics comes together with the elected official. This official may be local, county, state or federal. It is they who cast the votes which create our laws and policies. The influence of many all centers upon those who are elected. For most, being elected is the most sought-after position to hold. For others, it is the source of access to power. Regardless of the role you play, the business of politics centers around the elected.

2. The Political/Campaign Consultant.

Also known, sometimes, as the campaign manager in smaller campaigns, the role of the political consultant is to get you elected. They run the business of your campaign and craft your message while marrying it with good governing. They do the nitty-gritty work; so much of which you won't even know. They'll also try to dig up all of the skeletons that can be found on any opposition. They lurk quietly in the background, mostly choosing anonymity, so they can stealthily do whatever they need to do to get you elected. It is most important that you align yourself with a political consultant who shares your values and vision. After all, you must feel comfortable with this person. You will work very closely with them. In the classic sense, political consultants were known as ruthless. Perhaps some are. Not all. They are generally a reflection of their candidate. If you, the candidate, adhere strongly to certain values and principles, they will honor that. In my experience, if the consultant is ruthless, it is because the candidate allows it or is also ruthless.

3. The Political Party Leaders.

In years past, these were referred to as "Political Bosses". Today, we call them the political party leaders. They can be anyone who is in a position to broker deals, decide who is getting a party's nomination or raises the money needed for a campaign, or all of the above. In modern times, they are more likely to be your party chairpersons. The higher you are seeking to go in the political world, the more you will need these folks. It is they who will decide upon your political future. It is best to make friends with them and demonstrate your loyalty. Without them, you are going nowhere.

4. The Groupies.

Politicians can be perceived very much like celebrities. They sometimes attract groupies. Groupies are the people who are drawn to the spotlight, the power and the energy of politicians and campaigns. They pretty much just like to hang around and take selfies with the politicos. They may not offer any specific service. Most often they help to fill a room and create a buzz over a candidate. They are typically not out to hurt anyone and it is best to always acknowledge them and thank them. Ultimately, they like the attention they receive, and seem to enjoy the thrill of being in the middle of a campaign. And who doesn't enjoy having a perpetual group of people around you who always show up for you?

5. The Watchdogs.

Political Watchdogs are generally self-appointed. They grant themselves the title. They do not trust politicians and assume everything is either deceptive or nefarious in government. Therefore, it is their job to "watch" everything that goes on. Many actually look forward to being able to catch politicians doing anything wrong. That's their dream come true. My opinion over the years about Watchdogs is that many or most, deep down, want to be bigger players in the game. They would love to hold the very office they proclaim to watch. Sometimes they will seek office. Rarely do they win. You usually find them more at the local and county level. They rarely miss a meeting. They ask all sorts of questions at every meeting; questions that usually have a "gotcha" undertone. They then take to writing letters to the editor in which they always disagree with the politicos. They will almost never agree with anything proposed by any elected officials and believe everything to be a scheme of some sorts.

Watchdogs are a part of the process. Perhaps if all elected officials, everywhere, consistently did the right thing, there would be no need for them. In my experience, Watchdogs harp mostly on the negative. They seem to be pessimistic by nature. Perhaps this is why they do not trust anything put forth by politicians. However, because they generally focus upon the negative, they turn off the public and the politicians. I think if they changed their approach they would be far more effective. If, rather than trying to play "gotcha", they, instead, sought to offer ideas and contributions, they would have far more appeal and could effectuate change.

6. The Antagonists.

Every great story has a protagonist. But in order to have that protagonist, you need the antagonist, and politics is life's real great story. Also called political provocateurs, their role is to not just be against you or your position, it is to get under your skin and in your head. They literally antagonize their opponents and experience great joy in doing so. Again, in my experience, I have found that antagonists, like watchdogs, are often frustrated politicians. For whatever reason; whether it was lack of attention in childhood or an unhappy personal life, they derive great pleasure and satisfaction when causing trouble. I say this when referring to local political antagonists. The national ones are a different story. For them, it is how they make their living.

Like all frustrated politicians, they wind up precluding themselves from the process of which they so wish to be a part. They wind up frustrated in the end because mainstream people in politics avoid them. The best way to combat an antagonist is to ignore them. They are all about getting attention from the very people whom they antagonize, so the silent treatment will only make them go off the rails even more. However you do deal with them, best to not feed into what they say or do if it can be helped. And, by the way, a Watchdog can be an antagonist, but an antagonist may not also be a Watchdog.

7. The Professionals.

These are the lawyers, engineers, etc. who largely earn their living almost entirely on political contracts. Most of the money raised comes from these folks. Some are excellent fund raisers and bad lawyers, others might be great lawyers but not good fundraisers. And again, some are both! Either way, you need these people for they are the blood of political life and generally raise most of the money needed. Conversely, it is they who will earn most of the money on public contracts. My advice is to find professionals whom you like and with whom you feel a kinship. If you are in this for the long-term, you will find that they will stay with you. They can be of great help to you in so many ways and on many levels. You will need their advice, their guidance and their expertise. I have developed lasting friendships with many over the years. They make for great friends. Be sure to develop a level of comfort and seek those who share your values.

8. The Crazies.

We all know who they are. These are the ones we do our best to avoid on the street. They always want to tell us what we should be doing. The problem is that their ideas are ludicrous. But you cannot tell them that. Instead, you stand there, listening with one ear, hoping perhaps a meteor will strike, ending the conversation or your misery, or both. They will keep you longer than anyone else and they always follow up on their absurd ideas to see when you have "taken their advice". The thing to remember is that these folks rarely get attention from anyone else. But as politicians, we must listen to them. They are not bad people, per se. But they hang around, hang on and have the tendency to wipe your energy dry. It's important to be polite and always have somewhere else to go when you need to cut those conversations as short as possible.

9. The Volunteers.

Whether it is envelope stuffing, making phone calls, going door to door, setting up chairs or making coffee, these folks are the real life blood of any campaign. In general, these are members of your immediate and extended family, neighbors, retired folks and all-around good ole' fashioned ordinary citizens. They usually do not have a political agenda; at least nothing big or surprising. They enjoy playing a role in helping a candidate win. They are the grass roots. They are there to help you and will do almost anything if you ask them. In the great game of politics, it is they I always trusted most because they did not have an angle other than a care and concern for their community, district, etc. Take good care of these folks and treat them well. Never forget to thank them at every chance! Stay in touch with them after a campaign has ended; win or lose. When needed, they will always rise to the call.

10. The Ideologue.

The very nature of politics brings about those who cling undyingly to a political ideology regarding a specific issue or related issues. While in my experience they represent the minority of the politicos, it is they who help us find the middle. Ideologues generally define the extremes of the political landscape and, as such, are a part of the process.

Generally, they are not open to compromise and are more likely to cause dissension among the ranks. They are not interested in listening to opposing points of view, nor are they willing to give on their end. At all costs, they want their specific issue or issues to go their way; period. I have found that ideologues live in a very specific belief system. They absolutely believe in what they believe. While most middle of the road thinking people are rather fluid in their beliefs and open to other points of view, Ideologues generally are not.

Ideologues may stay in the political game forever but, in my experience, they accomplish very little. If and when they do get to hold a position of influence or power, they insist on their agenda being forced through at any cost. They crush and destroy anyone with opposing viewpoints, they are not open to debate, possess tunnel-vision and wind up driving mainstream people away from them. Even if they are successful in pushing through their ideological agendas, their lifespan of power is usually short due to the enemies they make. And enemies they do make. Lots of them! Because of this, they cause immense anger and resentment among others who then turn all of their energies toward the ultimate removal of such an ideologue. As a result, once ideologues no longer possess their position of power, there's not a person left in the establishment who will lift so much as a pinky for them.

I want to be clear that just because someone is an Ideologue, it does not negate the importance of their issue or cause. I discuss this point because the business of politics is power, influence and accomplishment in the course of good governing.

If an Ideologue truly wants to accomplish their agenda, they need to work with others and gain their favor in order to achieve their goal. If your goal is the moon, shoot for the stars, instead. Start off with a loftier goal so after you "negotiate", you still wind up with what you wanted in the first place. In other words, Ideologues would have a far greater success rate if they only learned to work with others.

COMMENTARY

While this list is not exhaustive, I find that most people in the business of politics fall into one or perhaps more of these categories. In fact, another category can be that of the political malcontent. A malcontent can even sometimes help by pointing out what is not going right or what needs correcting. Either way, my descriptions of each are more of a broad-based summary of each and by no means is meant to disparage anyone. In fact, I purposely describe the worst of each type of person in the hope of opening their eyes to why they may not have been very successful in this business. It can be said that politics is the best way to learn all about human nature. It attracts all types and kinds. If you do your best to follow the rules and have fun with it, it can be a grand experience of immense proportions along with great accomplishment for society. That is my wish for the reader.

4

The Political Speech and
Public Speaking

WHAT WOULD POLITICS be without a good old fashioned political speech? It is the crux of what politics is made of. A speech establishes your platform, it frames the issues and allows the constituents to get to know you. Becoming a good speaker takes practice. As one who coaches others on speaking, I often remind people not to get too overly caught up with content. For instance, don't stand before your audience and offer them your thirty-five point plan on reducing taxes. You will lose your audience no matter how good of a speaker you are. Instead, focus on style, delivery, energy, emotion and appearance. If you do, then you will learn how to convey your message most effectively.

According to most surveys, public speaking remains the number one thing people fear most. Death is second. So, to quote Jerry Seinfeld, that means, "People would rather be the person in the casket than the one giving the eulogy".

Let's face it, most speeches are boring. This is because few people truly understand the principles of a good speech. What's more, even fewer have had any kind of training. But even if your speaking skills are up to par, the speech itself could be the deal breaker if you manage to turn off your audience. In this section, I want to teach you all about the art of public speaking; the principles, the tips, tricks and psychological aspects, as well, that will help you to craft and deliver your message effectively.

I am asked all of the time, "How can I become a better public speaker?" The answer is somewhat similar to the old question, "How can I get to perform at Carnegie Hall?" The answer is same. Practice! I have witnessed many people evolve over a few years into truly good speakers. They improved through practice. And, if you are a politician, there's never a shortage of times where you can practice speaking. But to truly get the edge and take it up several notches, there are certain things you can learn which will take you there rather quickly.

Self-awareness: By the time you are done with this book, you will be hearing the words "self-awareness" in your sleep. That's because without it, you cannot improve upon yourself. You need the awareness of the areas of yourself which need improvement. For instance, do you rock back and forth when you speak? Do you use too many filler words such as "like" or "umm"? Do you fail to make eye contact with your audience? Perhaps you are too rigid and keep your arms straight at your sides? Maybe you are monotone? Whatever it is that you do, you can only know what you do through self-awareness and reflection. Self-awareness is the foundation on which all self-improvement is made. In fact, as I asked each of the previous questions with regard to your speaking, did you immediately ask yourself if you are guilty of any of them? Perhaps some, perhaps none? Either way, once you are aware of something, you can change it by giving it your attention.

Habit Creation: Public Speaking is a skill. Like any skill, you can learn it. The more you use the skill, the better you get. You can compare this to the learning and practicing of a new musical instrument or practicing a sport. Ultimately, the same thing is happening in your brain. It is re-wiring itself to better serve you when you engage in that skill the next time. We are each the sum total of all of our habits. Some good, some bad. The idea is to become aware of all of our bad habits and consciously work to create new, better habits. When it comes to speaking, this is no different. But in addition to creating new, good habits, we also want to be sure to slowly melt away those old, bad habits. So, here is what you will need to do to improve upon your speaking skills. Get a video camera of some sort. Today, that means your phone. You need to record yourself speaking. And as horrible and arduous as it may be, you need to watch yourself over and over and take note of anything that needs to change. Self-critiquing is never easy. Watching and listening to myself was always pure torture. But in the end, the results are superb.

Here are the tips that will help you to summon your inner Cicero:

1. Don't read a speech.

Listening to someone reading their speech is about as fun as counting ceiling tiles. In fact, that's what people will do when someone starts to read their speech. Here is my number one rule when it comes to speeches. If you learn this, you're off to a great start! *People will not remember what you said, but they will remember how they felt when you said it.* So, if you are thinking of giving that written speech that individually outlines your thirty-five-point plan to cut taxes, please spare your audience from that kind of torture and remember that <u>no one cares!</u> The "How" of what you want to do is not as important as the "Why" you want to do it.

Studies show that people will only remember about 10% of what they hear. But, they will always remember how they felt. This is because emotion is far more powerful than memory alone. People remember emotion. Think about yourself. When a song from your youth comes on the radio, do you not all of a sudden recall every emotion, good or bad, associated with the things in your life when that song originally was released? The same applies to a speech.

Let's take a look at one of the greatest speeches of all time: Martin Luther King, Jr.'s *I Have a Dream* speech. That speech was nearly seventeen minutes long. It is also arguably the most famous of speeches heard by nearly everyone on multiple occasions throughout their lives. Yet, ask anyone what Dr. King said and they will say, "*I have a dream*". He said far more than that, but most people will only remember his tag line (There is another reason for this, too, which I will explain later in this section). However, ask anyone how they feel or felt when they hear/heard it, and they will always tell you that it sends shivers down their spine. So, is it what he said or how he said it? It was his overwhelming, undying passion that comes right out and grabs any listener and pulls them right in. What MLK was able to do was create an incredibly strong sense of emotion for anyone who heard or continues to hear this epic, world-changing speech. In the end, people buy into _why_ you do or believe something, rather than what you believe.

What are you passionate about? For most politicians who are local, that passion may not be about civil rights or nuclear proliferation, but about taxes, litter, clean streets and better services. If you can conjure up your passion, you are on your way to a great speech. People buy into passion. It's why everyone loves a great drama; it draws forth powerful emotions. Emotions then drive momentum. So, when you are preparing to give a speech about any certain issue, find your passion. Then, instead of writing it out, jot down some key facts and figures. Most of all, turn it all into a story. Audiences always love a good story and research shows that they are far more likely to remember the story. If you can get away from a written script and talk about your passion and do so in a storytelling format, you are on your way. If you would like to read a personal account of how I got people excited about garbage, see the story box below.

Upon becoming the Commissioner of Public Works, in 2005, I set out to re-establish the township's recycling program which had fallen to the wayside. I knew I had to get the residents excited about recycling! I established an outreach which included the schools. I knew that if I wanted the adults to recycle, I had to get the kids of the township to buy-in. So, I toured the schools, spoke to the older students myself, and brought in a puppet show for the young children. I went to every local organization and spoke at their meetings. I even produced a local access program which aired constantly on the local cable channel.

I approached recycling from two different directions. First, I appealed to the taxpayer by letting them know how much garbage we were paying to remove each year and how recycling will make money, rather than cost us (At the time, recycling was very profitable). I then appealed to those who cared for the environment and illustrated how recycling helps to keep garbage out of landfills while helping our planet. I was now able to get nearly everyone on board with recycling for a reason which hit home for them.

Finally, I knew that as commissioner, I am responsible for setting the example. I would keep garbage bags and gloves in my trunk. Every time I drove past an area of town in which litter would pile up, I pulled over, got out and picked it up. Within a few weeks, word got around that the commissioner himself picks up litter. And because I was leading by example, all of a sudden, people's awareness of litter followed suit. It energized many people; adults and children, alike. Within a year, we lowered our garbage tonnage by three thousand tons, increased recycling by nearly that much; saved hundreds of thousands and made almost two hundred thousand! It was a turn-around of nearly one million dollars in a few years. But the best result of this all was the *fact that litter seemed to vanish and the streets were clean! The people began to notice and take pride in the cleanliness of their township. This is how important an elected official's role is and what it can accomplish when our intentions are right.*

The moral of this story is that as an elected official, you have the power to do great things when you believe in them and set an example for the public to follow! I was credited by the paper as the only person who was able to make garbage an exciting topic.

2. Less is more.

Now that you are weaning yourself off of written speeches and becoming familiar with passion and story-telling, here is the next important tip to grab and hold your audience. Keep it short! If the words you speak are not as important as the passion you share, then you want to keep that passion at all costs! You want people to leave there feeling great about you, your words, your energy, etc. In order to do so, we must employ the old adage from Vaudeville, *"Leave em' wanting more"*. Those old stage actors knew exactly what they were doing. You see, no matter how good a speaker you are, there is a limit to the time people will give you. When you use more time than you should, you lose your audience. But when you use less time, you leave them wanting more of you. Less is more. It's the reason diamonds, gold and fine jewels are worth a great amount of money. There is only so much of each.

A really good speech should be no more than five minutes. In fact, five minutes is far longer than you think in terms of speaking. But if you can deliver a rousing, passion-filled speech in five minutes or less, your audience will remember you, not the other speakers. They will remember your passion, energy and how you made them feel. Most importantly, they will want to see and hear you again! And in politics, we want to be in-demand! We want to be growing our base of supporters. Nothing causes people to follow others more than a shared passion coupled with great energy.

3. Your Voice and Using a Microphone.

Your voice is like an instrument. You can tune it, hone it and change the pitch and modulation. Of course, this takes practice. I am notorious for rarely needing a microphone. But most need one. And the fact of the matter is that there is nothing worse than listening to someone who does not know how to use a microphone. Too many stick it almost in their mouth, causing a very rough, static sound that is irritating to the ears of your audience. Others hold it too far away and the audience cannot hear what you say. Like anything else, you need to become familiar with the volume of your voice and practice with a microphone. In fact, if you can have someone you know stand in the back of the room and signal to you, they can let you know when you are too loud, too soft or just right. Eventually, you will be able to adjust your voice on your own.

4. Body Language and Gestures.

With plenty of practice and self-critique, you can learn how to properly gesture. Most communication is non-verbal; meaning that in addition to the words spoken, your body language, tone of voice and facial expressions make up the majority of a message. Learning how to take control over your body and facial expression takes time and practice. It also requires self-awareness. The greatest way to evolve yourself toward better body language is to ask someone to video you as you speak. Then, you can review the video as many times as necessary to critique everything you said and did. This is the kind of thing that is hard to teach in a book and can only come about through consistent awareness of and attention to your body language. Keep working at it and you will develop a keen ability to match your body with your words and emotions. Together, this is what makes for a great speaker. For those who truly want to evolve in this area, using a personal speaking coach is your best bet.

5. Eye-contact.

Making eye contact is a very powerful element of human interaction. It shows confidence, dominance (in some cases), truthfulness, respect and commands people to pay attention to you. Any time you address a crowd, you will want to be sure you are giving eye contact to everyone, at some point. One of the techniques I use when I coach speakers is what I call the "Clock Rule". Think of your audience as representing the top half of a traditional clock. The people on your left represent 9 o'clock to 11 o'clock. Those in the middle, in front of you, represent noon. And those to your right represent 1 o'clock to 3 o'clock. In order to be sure you are acknowledging everyone in your audience, start off by looking toward 9 o'clock. Then, slowly move your eye contact up and down, in order to make contact with people near you and those in the rear. Keep moving across the clock until you hit the far right side of the audience, or, 3 o'clock. Once you have done that, you can either work your way backward, or merely start off at 9 o'clock again.

When you first start to attempt to focus your attention upon all of these little things, it may seem daunting. But the more you do it, you wind up creating a new habit and your mind will wire itself to do these things every time without your needing to think about it. Just remember that every great speaker had lots of practice.

6. Cadence.

Cadence is defined as a modulation or inflection of the voice. Think of it as a drum beat. If you listen to the greatest of speakers, you will notice that their voice follows a specific beat. The idea of this is that it is easier for people to follow what you are saying when your speech flows with a certain beat in which each contains a small number of easily remembered words. President John F. Kennedy, as well as his father, Ambassador Joseph P. Kennedy, were notorious for speaking in a cadence. As you learn to create your own kind of cadence, you can also practice having your gestures align with the cadence of your speech which serves to underscore the important parts of your speech.

Any time you make an important point to your audience, pause. A pause is a subconscious signal to your audience that what you just said is very important and worthy of note. The longer the pause, the more important it is. In fact, one of, if not the longest pause I have ever witnessed in a speech was that of Prime Minister Benjamin Netanyahu of Isreal. In a very poignant speech to the United Nations, he paused for an entire 45 seconds as he stared down the audience. It seemed like a lifetime and caused anyone in the audience to feel highly uncomfortable, I'm sure. Netanyahu was angry, to say the least, about the state of anti-Isreali sentiments and lack of support among so many member nations. In what can only be described as the longest pause in speech history, his anger was visible in his eyes, but the pause made everyone realize just how angry he was. In fact, while he paused, he looked all around the audience, straight into their eyes. No one got away without experiencing his cold, hard stare. If you have not seen this, you can easily find this speech on Youtube. It is worth studying for its effective use of eye contact and pause.

So while you will want to have a good cadence during the majority of your speech, you most definitely want to pause when you make a very important point. The length of the pause will underscore the importance of your point.

7. The Rule of Three.

As we discussed already, people remember very little of what you actually say. If there are a few points, or even only one (Recommended), you want the audience to take away from your speech, then you will need to say it three times during the course of your speech. It takes three times before a person really will grasp your point or remember what you said. Again, this is why MLK said "I have a Dream" multiple times.

This was his hook. This was his takeaway. If you can come up with one or possibly two things you want your audience to take away from your speech, you must find the way to mention each three times throughout.

Important Points to Remember:

*Practice is the best way to improve your speaking skills
     *Avoid reading your speech
     *Learn how to use a microphone
     *Keep eye contact with your audience
     *Speak in a cadence and pause to make a point
     *Mention your main point at least three times.
     *Keep your speech short and leave the audience wanting more

5

Social Media: Your
Continuous Campaign

NOTHING HAS DONE more to change the political world than the advent of social media. It pretty much leveled the playing field by giving a platform to everyone to voice their opinions. And boy do they have opinions. Social media includes, but is not limited to, Facebook, Twitter and Instagram. You can also add YouTube to that list, as well. No matter the platform you use, whether one or all of them, you must be well-versed on all of the benefits and pitfalls to its use.

The first thing any politician needs to understand is that social media is an extension of who you are. In many cases, it will be the main venue in which people can learn all about you and peer into your life; personal, political or otherwise. This section could very well have been added to the chapter about developing your image later on. It is, after all, the greatest manner in which to develop, enhance, preserve or even destroy your image; depending upon how you use it. But, because so many public officials and others in the public eye seem to often make such bumbling mistakes, I had to give this its own chapter.

The first thing to understand about the Internet and all digital media is its permanency. Once you click that share or send button, it is out there for all to see, now and forever more. Even if you delete what you shared, someone else may have saved it. And if you are a politician, you can bet there will be people who save everything and anything you share just because they can. You can also rest highly assured that your political enemies are lurking in the background, checking out your social media shares more than your supporters. They wait for you to post that one thing that can be used to discredit, tarnish or otherwise, destroy you. All is fair in love, war and, of course, politics.

I will discuss each medium of social media by pointing out what it is good for, but also to make you very much aware of what it is not good for. So, start to think about your own social media and what may or may not be on it, in it or attached to it; and always be thinking how you would use it against you if you were on the other side. If you learn to think how your political enemies think, you will begin to understand the destructive nature of social media and start being very careful about what you share.

FACEBOOK

If Facebook has taught me one thing, it is that many people do not work. I don't mean that they do not have a job. I mean that they have one, they just don't seem to work all that much. All day long, some people post and post and post. Others lurk and stalk. Some love to play those annoying games and send you invites, while still others love to use many of the apps that morph your face into some old movie star or person from history.

The point is, Facebook has become the main forum for nearly every person in our society. Regardless of age or gender, there they are and there they dwell. If you are a cute animal, it's the fastest and easiest way to become an animal celebrity. Nearly every politician I know has a Facebook page. But for most of them, it is their personal Facebook page which is their first mistake. An elected official or anyone deeply involved in the world of politics should maintain two separate Facebook accounts. One can be reserved for your friends and family, the other to be used as your official page for the position you hold, or are seeking to hold. In other words, your public persona.

FACEBOOK FAN PAGES

The proper way to maintain a Facebook presence and communicate with your fans/constituents/public, etc. is to have a "Fan Page". This means that members of the public who want to follow you would click the "Like" button, not send a "friend request". In order to have a Fan page, you need a regular profile from which to create it. This will help you to separate your public from your private life. Frankly, you really do not have much of a private life in politics. But either way, the regular profile you set up could bear some sort of moniker or, shortened name. It is common for law enforcement to use their first and middle name and leave off their last. So, if you are in public life, your personal Facebook page should be as private as you can make it, while your Fan page is your public forum.

Once you have established your Fan page, this is your platform to share only those things which apply to the position you hold or the one you seek. It should only consist of your public persona. If you do share anything regarding your family life or personal life, it must be done in such a way as to be perfectly staged to not reveal anything truly personal. For instance, photos of your vacation and family bar-b-que should be reserved for your personal Facebook page. However, a public bar-b-que at which you appear in your capacity as a candidate or elected official is acceptable. A Fan page is a great way to stay in touch and communicate with your people. Just make sure that everything you do post has something to do with your official capacity or campaign.

Another valuable thing regarding Fan Pages on Facebook is that you can pay to boost your posts as well as air commercials you may make. As more and more people get their news online, and fewer watch traditional TV, the political commercial has now begun its move to include every aspect of social media. Facebook is best for this!

As for your personal Facebook page, I highly recommend that you still be extremely careful as to what you post. Even if you set the highest security and privacy settings to ensure your photos and information are not able to been seen by anyone other than those you choose, it is not worth the chance. Here is the litmus test: any time you are about to share something, ask yourself these questions:

- *Does it help support the image I have established?*
- *Will this be something that, if it were to appear in a political ad, would hurt my image?*
- *Is what I am sharing something of which in ten years I will be proud?*

If you have any questions or doubts, then err on the side of not sharing it. Remember, if you really want your cousins to see your vacation pics, you can always e-mail them. You just have to trust that your cousins will keep the photos to themselves. Photos of you dancing, holding alcoholic beverages while donning a bathing suit and wearing a lei would be great optics for your political adversary to use in a mailer to demonstrate how much of a party person you are. Of course, it is your right to be a party person. Frankly, you should be able to do whatever you want. But, this is politics. If you are willing to take a chance on anything being used against you, then you have only yourself to blame.

TWITTER

I have seen more careers in politics and the business world end in 140 characters or less. Twitter is a very unique platform.

I personally have no use for it, yet I have one. The idea is that Twitter is like a stream of consciousness for people to post what is on their minds at the moment. The problem is that what is on your mind, in many instances, needs to be filtered and vetted prior to Tweeting it. Unless you are a high-profile politico who wants to engage with others on various topics and issues, I do not recommend using it. Of course, you can plan out your Tweets and use them to link back to things on your Facebook or YouTube accounts. However, you really will not get much traction and it is hardly worth the effort. Twitter is for people who use it regularly, on a daily basis, to engage with others. If you are running for office, I recommend very limited public statements regarding an issue that have not been thoroughly edited, evaluated and vetted.

Again, stop and think before you Tweet. Ask yourself those same questions as above. I always believe that playing it safe in politics is the best course of action which yields the greatest long-term results. Twitter is definitely not for the amateurs. On the other hand if you want to play the role of antagonist and provocateur, then by all means, Tweet away! For the rest of you, play it safe.

One last important thing regarding Twitter is that you should never allow a staff member or assistant to use it for you. Unlike sharing approved photos and stories on Facebook, Twitter is a stream of consciousness platform. Only you should be the one to decide upon what to say in those 140 or fewer characters. And even you must be very careful. People in public life get in trouble every day for Tweeting things they should not have.

INSTAGRAM

A safer, friendlier platform is Instagram. It focuses mostly on pictures and not really on written content. Of course, it is loaded with Memes, so those could just as easily get you into trouble. But as for photos, stick to a professional appearance and don't post those shirtless or scantily-clad beach pics. Keep the alcohol out of the photo and stay as neutral as possible. Just keep asking yourself if what you are posting can in any way be used against you. Remember, this is politics, so if they cannot use something against you, they will just make it up. But if you play nicely in the game with others, they will generally play rather nicely with you. But there's no guarantee to that. There are always the exceptions.

YOUTUBE

What most people do not know is that YouTube is the second largest search engine, second only to Google; who happens to own YouTube. If you want to learn about anything or anyone, just search YouTube. Someone, somewhere, will have made or posted a video on the subject.

YouTube is a great resource for sharing your video content which, for a politician, is your greatest tool. Once you record and post a video, you can then share it on your Facebook page, Twitter and even Instagram; albeit a shorter version. What's more, it has never been easier to record your own videos than it is now. You can easily use your phone or the built-in cam on your computer. Just make sure to review the video a few times before you post it. Again, you want to make sure you do not say or portray something in a way that can come back to haunt you. I highly recommend that you ask someone you trust to view it, as well, in order to get an outside opinion.

In addition to uploading your Videos to YouTube, you should use Facebook video and separately upload it to Facebook. The reason for this is because Facebook uses lots of crazy logarithms. They do not like to send people to another site. And since Facebook does not own YouTube, it tends to not show those videos to everyone. But, on the other hand, they love to promote their own video platform and will be sure to show it to more people. And, they'll make you pay if you want to reach a larger audience.

PODCASTS

Another great tool for getting your platform out there is to start your own podcast. A podcast, if you do not know, is like your own radio show. A small investment if about $90 on a Blue™ microphone and you will sound as good as a professional. Many politicians have their own podcasts as it gives them their own platform to get into the issues and discuss what's on their minds. It also is a great way for people to get to know you. You can have other guests on and use it as a way to cross-market yourself to other people's listeners. New York's legendary mayor, Fiorello LaGuardia, famously read the comics each weekend on the radio to the children. President Franklin D. Roosevelt used radio to deliver his fireside chats to the nation. And countless other political figures over the years have all used radio as a means of communicating their ideas to the public. It's a great deal of fun and, like all other things on social media, can be shared on all of your platforms; therefore grabbing as many listeners as possible. If you do it regularly, you will build a strong following of listeners who will also share and promote your show to their friends.

MANAGING SOCIAL MEDIA

I do not manage my own social media. As a business person and public figure, I have people who do that for me. I highly recommend getting a professional company to handle your social media for you. It does not have to be expensive and can be customized in any way you want, such as, one post a day, every other day, once per week, etc. Anything you want can be done for you. In fact, the two guys who handle my social media now have begun to handle the social media for politicians and campaigns. So, should you want a wonderfully reliable company to do it for you, just visit Adam and Nick Buongiovanni at TriplexMediaSpecialists.com. Of course, most politicians are local and most likely have a small, if any, budget. In that case, see if you can get a family member or someone else to handle it for you if you do not have the time. Just make sure they read this book and this chapter first.

Whether you handle it yourself or retain a company to do so, you still want to be the one who engages and answers the messages and comments. I always answer all of my messages and comments personally. No matter who handles it, you still need to be in the mix of it. So the posts and shares can be done for you, but the message must always be yours.

6

Warnings and Admonishments

IN MY QUEST to highlight the well-known negative perceptions of some politicians, and my desire to raise awareness
of the importance of being a role model and representative of
good government, I offer the following.

I have witnessed more than my fair share of politicians who
rose to the top only to come tumbling down. I actually have
had multiple first-hand experiences in this matter in which I
knew, personally, the once-mighty fallen. This allowed for me
to take notice of the common themes among them which led
to their fall. Whatever roll you play in the world of politics, no
matter how high you may rise, there are certain things to avoid
which have the potential to lead to your becoming a political
Humpty Dumpty. There are plenty of icebergs in the political
sea. If you want to last in this business, you need to spot these
icebergs long before they evolve into a head-on collision. It is

best to examine yourself to be certain you are not making one of these potentially deadly mistakes.

I've seen so many talented, highly intelligent individuals—who should never have lost their power—lose it all. Overnight. It is very rarely because someone out-smarted them or out-strategized them. It's usually because they fell into one or more of the following and made some very bad decisions. So how does this happen? How can you avoid this from happening to you? Read on and see how many of the following you or your fellow politicos may have committed.

BEWARE OF THE BUBBLE

Politics is the business of power. Power should, ideally, be used effectively and for great purpose. In order to preserve that power, you need to be in touch with what people are thinking. You need to keep a finger on the pulse of everyone and everything around you. You must have tentacles which reach into multiple streams of groups and information. Far too often, I have seen politicos wind up in a small bubble in which they only speak to and hear from a small circle of people. The problem is that these small circles of people generally tell you what you want to hear. In actuality, they only tell you what 'they' want you to hear; or what they want you to know. We must realize that those around us may also be trying to preserve their own power. In due course, you will lose touch with the people and you will not be aware that your ship has hit an iceberg until it is already sinking.

I am sure you have heard the saying, "The Emperor wears no clothes". The people around you in your bubble will most likely never tell you that you are "naked". Many politicos are surrounded by "yes-men" or, more rarely, "yes-women" who are afraid to inform their leader that he or she is on a losing course. Never be afraid to hear the truth. To succeed in politics in the long-term, you must be in touch and realistic. Always keep some people in your circle who speak frankly and honestly when needed. Call upon people with various and different viewpoints. Doing so allows you to pivot as needed and take evasive action when something is headed toward the path of failure.

This is why a successful politician's greatest asset are the people. Stay close to them, listen carefully and treat them well. They will demonstrate that same loyalty right back at you.

DON'T HURT OTHER PEOPLE'S FAMILY MEMBERS

Ah, revenge. That seemingly sweet elixir craved by so many within the power-brokering business. After all, what's better than such a succulent dish of revenge served over a serving of your enemies? The vengeance to which I am referring is using your political power to hurt the family members and friends of your political enemies. Well, while it may be personally satisfying, it will always cost you your power in the end. This is politics. Rule number one is to never take things personally. Politics is about taking a side and fighting for it. You will face people on opposite sides. But that should not cause you to become vengeful. I have yet to meet a politico who has never felt he or she were wronged at some point or another. It happens. It's part of the business. The problem with vengeance is that it becomes all-consuming and begins to cloud your thinking and your vision. The public does not care who wronged you, so if and when you begin to put your energies into getting back at those who may not have supported you, or worse, you decide to go after their family members and friends, you have begun to sing your own political swan song.

The worst mistake you can make which will guarantee your political demise is to go after people personally. Let's say a fellow politico who worked against your candidacy has a relative who works for the town, county, etc. If you win and then decide to use your position to go after that relative purely because their family member did not support you, you will suffer the consequences in the end. You may win in the short-term, but lose in the long-term. Never, repeat, never go after someone's family. You will only entice, empower and energize them, their entire family and all of their friends to spend all of their energy to get rid of you. Why would anyone want to risk that? And yet, they do.

The other issue is that once you become consumed with revenge, people around you slowly start to wonder if they may be next. This leads to your losing people in your organization because your objectives are no longer positive or constructive. Instead, they are negative and destructive. And energy like that will never attract people to you. It only causes them to flee.

THE BIG EGO

Everyone has an ego. In politics, you will perhaps find larger ones than usual. But, nevertheless, ego plays a huge roll in politics. The key is to keep that big ego in check. Nothing can cloud your political astuteness more than an overblown ego. The worst egos usually accompany a certain amount of Narcissism and/or sociopathy. We all know certain people like that. Generally, they wind up climbing to the top of the top very quickly through their cunning, manipulative and intimidating ways. But, they almost always fall. It might take some time, but trust me, they will fall. When we learn to spot these personalities early on, we can work to prohibit these toxic personalities from advancing any farther. This takes time and great wisdom to be able to spot these personalities early on. Chances are, you will have been the victim of one, first, before you fully understand this type of personality within the political realm.

On the other hand, a smart politician knows that his or her job is to build everyone around them up; to motivate and encourage them. That is how you build your base of support. You must earn their loyalty by showing them you will cover them and protect them at all costs. You need to demonstrate your devotion to the public good. If you make it all about yourself and forsake others who have helped you— merely using people as you need them—you will ultimately lose your influence and lose the support and respect of your followers.

And one final piece of advice coming from a half-Irish politician is to never, ever take yourself too seriously. You need to be able to laugh at yourself. JFK had the unique ability to engage in self-deprecation. The public loves it when you laugh at yourself. You demonstrate that you are real and down-to-earth. As my grandfather, Nicholas Carella, quipped, "Self-praise stinks". If you are going to praise, praise others. And if you are going to be praised, only be prosed by others. Of course, that means to do things that are praiseworthy.

TAKE NOTHING FOR GRANTED

Never assume anything. Don't assume you have someone's support without asking. Do not assume a prospective problem or issue will go away. There's an expression which says "From little acorns do big Oak Trees grow." There are countless little things that can either grow into something larger, or fester into something serious. It is important to always be on the lookout for anything or anyone which might not be a big deal at the moment, but has the potential to become something bigger or problematic. And most important, do not create issues where none should be.

Be alert and vigilant. Just when everything seems calm and you feel your reelection is a guarantee, just remember the Titanic. The waters were as calm as glass, but they never saw the iceberg coming until it was too late. Whether it is a disgruntled resident, a group of residents starting to complain about a certain issue or internal issues with your own people, be ready to take action immediately and nip whatever it is in the bud. It could be anything. Your job is stay ahead of everything and get out in front of it; whatever it may be.

COMMENTARY

The path to success in politics is easier than you may think. If you have good people skills, are reliable and consistent, can work with others and have a great personality built on a foundation of good character, you will most assuredly advance in the great world of politics. If you do not, you will not. It's that simple. There is a quote of mine which I use in my regular teachings which applies to all of life:

> *"If you are kind, people will overlook your flaws. If you are unkind, even your strengths will be judged harshly"*
>
> BRIAN HAGGERTY

7

Developing and Managing
Your Public Image

PERCEPTION IS REALITY and politics is all about perception. A successful politician works very diligently and carefully to develop a certain image that establishes their brand, while setting a standard of accomplishment. In a previous chapter, I discussed social media and how it can either establish and enhance your image, or hurt and tarnish it.

If you take a look at national politicians, they are no different, in many cases, than movie stars. They are all highly self-aware people who have worked for many years on polishing, perfecting, refining and building their individual image. Everything from the clothes they wear to the way they walk is carefully crafted to portray confidence and power. If you have ever been in the presence of someone high up on the political ladder, you have most certainly noticed that they have that certain something.

You, too, can develop that same "something". First, you need the desire to do it. Second, you need the awareness to critique every area of yourself. Then, you need to put the conscious practice into changing the areas of yourself as needed. Things such as posture, your gait and even your grammar are all areas on which high-level politicians have worked with great effort. But in addition to the manner in which you walk, how you speak and how you carry yourself is the energy you put forth to others; coupled with your over-all personality, people skills and actual accomplishments. I have always felt that local politicians have far more of an ability to get something accomplished. This is mostly because there is less bureaucracy with which to deal. So, why not use your position well and work toward actually getting something done. This is what the people want and expect from their elected leaders.

Let's take a look at areas regarding your image.

YOUR ATTIRE

If you were elected to office, you are among a select few. When holding an office, you represent that office. However, it is not "your" office, but that of the people. In order to maintain respect for such an office, you should act and dress accordingly. When you are well dressed, you feel different. People treat and respond to you differently. Your attire has a psychological effect on how you perceive yourself as well as how others perceive and treat you. If you wear sweat pants, sneakers and a baseball cap, you will not command the respect that you would if you dress well.

I do not mean to say that you should attend a summer bar-b-que in a suit and tie. What I am saying is that your appearances in public should be marked by appropriate attire. If the occasion does not call for a suit for a man or a pant suit or dress for a woman, at least be sure to wear clothes that are clean, pressed and fall into the category of "smart casual". However, for any official meetings or gatherings, always be dressed in Business Attire. Nothing bothers me more than when I see a councilperson attend an official meeting in anything less than business attire.

Oh, and one last thing. Men, please shine your shoes! A nice suit is eclipsed by worn-out, scuffed shoes.

YOUR POSTURE AND GAIT

Nothing sends a stronger, more powerful non-verbal message about you than the manner in which you carry yourself. What do your posture and gait say about you? What non-verbal or subliminal messages do they convey? Do they convey confidence, strength, vigor and approachability? Or, do they convey weakness, indecisiveness and standoffishness? Body language speaks volumes about who and what we are. On the stage of politics, it is the stuff Shakespeare is made of. With some awareness and practice, you can alter or change every aspect of your body language to convey the proper messages. Let's explore a few of the basic areas here.

- Do you stand straight? And if you do, do you do it always; even when you walk? Studies show that when it comes to confidence, you can fake it till you make it. Standing tall, walking with your head level with the ground and swinging your arms in just the right way will not only make you look important and confident, it will make you feel it!

- When you walk, make sure your feet are pointed straight ahead. If you have a duck walk or are pigeon toed, you can consciously practice forcing yourself to walk with your feet pointed directly in front of you. After all, the way we walk is the result of having always walked that way. Our body is doing what it has always done. But if you consciously start to change it, over time, it will remake your walk. This, of course, assumes that you do not possess any physical challenge which would impede your walking.

- Be sure to look out and around you. Smile and always acknowledge people either with your eyes, a head nod or a wave; depending upon your proximity to others. But make sure you smile as that is what makes you and others feel good.

- Watch videos of presidents and senators. Pay attention how they walk, what they do with their arms and how they acknowledge people when they enter a room. No reason to reinvent the wheel. If you practice doing this and feel comfortable, you can do the same.

If you really want to learn presence, all you need to do is go to YouTube and watch videos of famous politicians or movie stars.

Study everything about what they do with their bodies when the camera is on them. The two presidents I believe had the greatest walk, gait and presence are JFK and Ronald Reagan. In my opinion, they epitomized what it means to act, walk, dress and carry oneself like a president. Even if you are only a local elected official, there is nothing wrong with looking like a star and exuding all sorts of confidence and energy. Either way, it will increase your being noticed and admired by the people and will make you stand out.

Here is something national politicians do whenever they walk up on a stage; whether during a rally or public event. If you notice, they always point and wave at people in the audience as if they know these people. This is called Phantom Waving. They actually do not know anyone in the audience and frankly are not pointing or looking at any one person. This is done because it makes the politician look important as well as makes them look like they have friends in every city they tour. Like I said early, politics is theater and perception is reality.

TAKING PHOTOS

While some may find this information amusing, it is, nonetheless, what is done among some of the most successful politicos. Photo taking is an enormous part of being a politician. Nearly everything is a photo op and a photo is a lasting record of the event. In years past, not everyone had a camera. Today, everyone does. So, it's a little more daunting to beware of the cameras in the room. But when the time for a photo arises, here are a few things to keep in mind in order to best control how you look in photos.

- Find out which side of your face is best for photography. Most have a better side. Be aware of this so that when you do stand for a photo, and before you take your place for that photo, stand in such a place and in such a manner as to have your better side facing the camera.

- Put down anything you are holding before taking a photo. If it is a dinner, put down the drink. If you are holding something, put it down to free up your arms.

- Height seems to matter on the big stage of politics, so unless you are the tallest person, avoid standing next to someone who towers above you. This is more for men than for women, because women are not generally judged by their height and can wear heels if need be. A little trick to appear taller in photos is to stand slightly closer to the camera than everyone else. If done right, the effect it will produce in the photo will be to make you appear larger and taller than everyone else.

- Try to eat before you go to dinners or rallies where food is served. There will be guests who will gorge themselves on free food. But as a politico, you are not there to eat, but to be constantly meeting, greeting and speaking with people. If you are too busy eating like it is your last meal, you will not be able to engage with people. And, in addition, you don't want to risk food or salad being caught in your teeth and showing up in that high-resolution photo with your big toothy grin on parade. Remember that any bad photo of you can be used in your opponent's campaign literature. In addition to eating lite, keep a small mirror and a tooth pick or something similar in your pocket and keep watch of things which may get caught in your teeth.

- Get used to smiling. Studies show that the very first thing people notice about us is our smile. Make sure it is a natural smile, not a put-on. Smiling actually tricks your brain into releasing endorphins into the bloodstream which will make you feel physically better. In addition, mirror neurons in our brains cause us to feel good merely by seeing someone else smile. So, in the words of the Honeymooners character, Ed Norton, "Show em' the old Liberace".

- Pay close attention to whomever it is you are posing with for a picture. I am not referring to members of the public, per se, but to other people who are involved in the political world one way or another. If it is someone who is controversial in any way, you may want to either not take a photo or stand as far away in the photo from that person as possible. Remember, if a political consultant can use a photo of you with someone who is the current "enemy" of the public or who is controversial, you can be assured it will be used in a mailer against you.

- Avoid putting on any silly hats and taking a photo. If the hat makes you look like a cartoon character, again, it can be used in campaign literature. If your political enemies want to make you look cartoonish, giving them the tools with which to do so is your own fault.

POLITICAL OPTICS

Political Optics is an expression which was tossed around by a certain governor after what became seemingly the worst-case of political optics ever; the now iconic photo of Governor Chris Christie sitting on his beach chair when the beaches were closed to the public. I personally feel he knew what he was doing and did it intentionally, but I also do not think he expected it to become an internet meme for the ages. Knowing the governor, I don't think he loses sleep over any of it. Either way, he introduced the word "political optics" to the public during the press conference, afterward, in which he said he didn't care about political optics. Granted, as of this writing, he is in his final months as governor and probably is done with holding office. But that photo will undoubtedly define him most likely forever.

Whether you are a local councilperson, a mayor or hold a higher office on a county or state level, your appearance is important. The higher you go, the more important your appearance. However, I am a strong proponent that no matter how local, small or insignificant you think a position may be, you are still a public official and should behave and carry yourself as such. You never know where politics may take you. Always assume that you very well may run for a larger, higher office. And always assume that if you do, you can rest assured everyone will be looking back at everything you ever did previously. You want to be sure that if anyone were to look back, you always looked professional and in command.

A good, clean appearance, coupled with great people skills and solid character are the ingredients for success as a politician.

MY THOUGHTS ON ALCOHOL AND HOLDING ADULT BEVERAGES

In this matter, my advice is to never hold an alcoholic beverage in your hand when out in public. In fact, if anything, hold a bottle of water. You want to avoid anyone ever assuming—or your enemies saying—that you drink too much. Whether it is one drink or ten, no one will know. But holding that drink in your hand, then being photographed, only serves to allow others to define you. In my lifetime, I have been around far too many political office holders who drink far too much in public at parties or events. In fact, sometimes it is obvious they have been drinking rather heavily. Whether they want to believe it or not, people will talk about them. Do this enough, and people will say, "He or she drinks too much". That's a bad thing for a politician. While you are free to drink if you wish, you are only opening yourself up to something which can be used to define you and used against you when you do so publicly. It can demonstrate a lack of control. It could fuzz your thinking and speech just enough to take you off balance. Your enemies will be sure to get the whisper campaign out there that you are a drinker and always drunk; even if that is not true. This is why perception is reality.

Be responsible. But also recognize that office holders—and those seeking office—are held or should be held to a higher standard. I personally enjoy wine. However, when in any official capacity or out in public, I never had a sip. I wanted to be sharp and in control at all times.

COMMENTARY

While image is so very important to your success in politics, it in no way should be valued more than substance. Be of good character and always do what is right and best. Ultimately, the substance of who you are is what matters most. These are merely tools to guide and assist you in developing the self-awareness of the areas in which improvements can be made.

8

Mindfulness and a Healthy
Emotional Intelligence

YOU MAY HAVE heard the word Mindfulness being floated around. In fact, it appeared on the cover of TIME Magazine in the summer of 2017. This is the corporate world's latest approach toward helping their employees develop Emotional Intelligence, or "EI.". I bring this point up because I am a very strong proponent of self-reflection and believe that within the realm of politics, our decisions should not be made in haste, but rather through thoughtful reflection, consideration and analysis of all sides and ramifications.

In addition to allowing yourself time to think and reflect on your decisions, this also helps you to develop more self-control as well as work at developing your intuition which, in politics, can be a most valuable tool.

Every day, a politician faces challenges, decisions and meets new people. I am sure you have met people who seem to give you a bad feeling in your gut. That is your natural intuition resulting from the 100 billion neurons in your gastrointestinal tract. Intuition is an inner guidance system that has its roots in our evolution. It is nature's way of detecting and sensing impending danger; just as we can see in every animal in nature. By becoming increasingly aware of the feelings we receive regarding people, issues or events, we increase our EI and can hopefully minimize our exposure to harmful people and/or things.

Therefore, it would a good idea for you to take a certain time slot each day. Twenty minutes is sufficient. Make sure you are in a quiet place. Review your day, the things you did, the people with whom you spoke, etc. Make note of how you feel when you bring certain things to mind. Is there a feeling of apprehension in your gut about something? If so, you may want to examine the subject further. Is there something which causes you continuous anger or aggravation? If so, allow yourself to feel the emotion and then try to find out why it triggers you in a negative way. On the other hand, if you feel lighthearted and confident about something, it may be your intuition telling you that it does not sense any impending danger or discord.

Understand that self-reflection is another tool to use to both improve upon yourself and discover what makes you tick. It also allows for us to make more reasoned decisions about everyone and everything we come into contact. The only way to sharpen your senses is to work at it. Keep comparing the results of your decisions with how you felt about that decision at the time you made it. After a while, you'll get better at doing it. It will give you an increased amount of wisdom and will serve you very well.

So when faced with decisions such as a platform or issue on which to run; running mates, policy or even running for a different or higher office, self-reflected, wise and evolved choices will increase your success. But fast, rash and slip-shod decisions made in the moment can harm you greatly. It could also lead to your political demise. Learn to see things from every angle. Examine things through the eyes of others. Ask yourself questions regarding the ramifications of your decision. Before long, you will have developed a tremendous Emotional Intelligence from which you can improve every single aspect of your life.

9

The Good, the Bad and the Ugly

ONE THING THAT is certain is that politics is one of the most fascinating and exciting of endeavors. Of course, there are many sides to the world of politics. Some good, some bad and sometimes, even ugly. It's not always for the faint of heart. But if you have that fire in your belly and do the right thing, be aware of the good and the bad. Here are some descriptions of those sides as I see them.

THE GOOD

To me, there is nothing more exciting than being in the midst of politics. It is the source of accomplishment, achievement and influence. Those of you seasoned politicos know the feeling we get on election night. When a win occurs, our minds are flooded with the potential of what can be. Every single politico truly wants to make a difference. It is very rewarding and a great honor to be in a position of influence. There are many great things one can do, and a good many people one can help. You will meet all sorts of amazing, exciting and unique individuals. You are in a position to help others by getting the wheels of progress in motion.

If you are successful at politics, as described in this book, you are, in essence, part of a larger group. You might even say part of a larger family. After all, with all of the contacts, friends and associates you make, nearly anything is a phone call away should you need the advice or assistance of others. Life is about networking and politics is certainly the largest network there is. As long as you stay true to your core beliefs and not forget that you serve the public, you will find it a most fulfilling endeavor.

The Bad

As with anything in life, it is the contrasts which put everything in perspective. Aside from all of the good that can come from politics; all of the excitement and accomplishment, there is also the bad. For one thing, you wind up with very little time for yourself and your family. Depending upon the office you hold, you may only get to spend time with your family once, perhaps twice, a week. If you have young children, this is even more difficult. The biggest cost in politics is time. While it is well spent if you spend it wisely, it also can be all-consuming. A night off is rare. And if you are in the middle of a campaign, knocking on doors, meeting people all day, your lack of sleep will also be an issue. Ultimately, it is the business of blood, sweat and tears and lots of each.

In addition, there is a great deal of drama which, if you don't handle it properly, will also consume you and could get you in the middle of trouble. Rumors, insecurities, egos and agendas seem to line up everywhere you may look; especially during campaign season. And for as many new friends as you can make, there are ample opportunities to make new enemies. But if you follow the rules of this book, you can reduce the number of those enemies and, at best, keep them as political enemies, not personal.

THE UGLY

As any politico knows, once you enter the game, you are, sadly, fair game. This is also what scares so many people away from the political realm. If you run for office, expect to be attacked. This is usually hardest for family members of political candidates. After all, seeing someone you love viciously attacked can be very difficult. The attacks go beyond what is written in political flyers. That's actually the easy stuff. It's the dirty little scoundrels who lurk anonymously online, or use the old fashioned whisper campaign to spread the most horrific rumors about you. Prepare to be accused of things that you have never dreamed of. You might be accused of being an alcoholic; even if you barely drink. Perhaps they'll say you have an illegitimate child or you are having an affair. It gets even worse than that. Use your imagination.

If not thoroughly prepared for this, some may crumble under such false accusations. But that is exactly why the bottom feeders, as I call them, do such things. They want to get in your head, intimidate you and chase you out of the game. Many towns have their own anonymous forums where insiders post all day and night about everyone they don't like. It's the modern version of what I referred to as the classic "Whisper Campaign". When they have nothing on you, they just make it up. They know they cannot put it in literature and they are actually cowards at heart. So, they resort to quietly saying things like, "Well, you know he's got a drug problem", or "She belongs to weird, crazy sex clubs".

Think of the worst thing you can accuse someone of doing, and they say something worse. Does it work? Well, that depends. A political novice may fall under the stress. But seasoned politicos know that the only thing to do is ignore it. In my town, I pretty much know who the main people are who do these things. I never paid any attention, nor did I care what was written. It's all childish nonsense being perpetrated by very fearful, insecure people who usually have a great deal at stake. If the bottom feeders are attacking you in the worst way you can imagine, it's because they fear you the most. Don't even read those types of forums or give it any energy. Nothing they say or do will either get you a vote or cause you to lose a vote. I have seen various people be incessantly attacked on anonymous boards and win in a landslide, time after time. So, the moment you feel you need to speak out or answer any of this dribble, you immediately elevate what is written and give it importance and attention.

People who are apolitical are not paying attention to the nonsense, so why bring attention to it. Remember, when you just ignore it, it does not work on you. And, it annoys them.

10

Thoughts and Musings About Politics

A s I MENTIONED in the introduction, I did not wish to focus upon strategy or the elements of campaigning. There are plenty of books and resources for those topics. Ultimately, your long-term success and staying power in politics will depend upon your likeability and achievements. Your image, your presence and how people feel about you will determine your success. Win or lose, you can be assured of having made the relationships and connections with others that will always give you access to power. Use that power wisely and do great things for the people.

This last chapter contains a bunch of unrelated musings and thoughts which I wrote out in the course of preparing for this book. None seemed to fit into any specific chapter, so I thought it best to just put them here for you to read and absorb.

One may have nothing to do with the other, but all are principles or pointers worth learning and remembering.

- *When you win, you act graciously. When you lose, you act graciously. The public expects their representatives to set an example of decorum and honor. Regardless of how you may personally feel about someone, you must always be gracious toward them. A politician will win and lose. But his or her staying power is rooted in his or her ability to get along with and work with others*

- *The most successful politicians are those who are accessible, do favors and build bridges. And the best of them know the real secret: do favors for those who did not support you. This way, you turn them into your supporter. It is better to make a friend out of an enemy than to battle them.*

- *Politics is the business of helping people. Ask yourself this question: If you are a moderate, mainstream thinker, for whom would you vote? The person whom you can call if in need of a favor, or the person who will not, or does not, do favors? Obviously, you will support the person who does favors. There are many times I vote for someone with whom I share few political views. But, I know them personally, I like them and I know that they are someone on whom I can count if need be.*

- *I have always wondered why everyone seems far more interested in national or state politics, rather than their own town. Ultimately, with few exceptions, what happens on a national level has little effect on the average person. Instead, what*

*happens in your own town has a major impact on your home's
value, your school district and your over-all quality of life.*

This story is to offer some insight into how to deal with members of the public when they call upon you to help with a situ-
ation with which they are dealing:

ALWAYS OFFER SOMETHING

*In my first elected term as a commissioner in my township, I became the
Director of Public Works. Sixteen years earlier, my father had held the
same position. Unlike a councilperson whose responsibilities are purely
legislative, a commissioner is also an executive and has sole direction
over his or her department.*

*The department of public works is integral to nearly everything in
a township. It includes the water and sewer services, streets, curbs, sidewalks, trees, garbage, recycling and engineering. It is, as I like to call it,
the 'favor' department. Ultimately, all you do are favors for the residents
who call upon you. It is perfect from a political standpoint because you
touch so many residents and have the ability to help or assist them.*

*I succeeded a prior commissioner who was not very responsive to the
public. Within my first month, I received a slew of letters and phone
calls from residents who had been waiting on things for many years.
Tree trimmings, broken sidewalks, potholes, etc; small things which did
not require much to get done. I spoke to each and every resident who
were hoping against all hope that I — the new commissioner—would
help them. And help them, I did. I would instruct the superintendent
to schedule the work requested immediately. After years of getting no*

response from the prior commissioner, the residents were shocked and delighted to see action take place within one or two days of speaking to me. To this day, I saved each and every letter they sent to thank me after the work was completed.

Sometimes, the request from a resident was something larger, such as the paving of an entire street. A project of that size is a capital project requiring the township to bond the expense. No single commissioner can do so and the board must decide, as a whole, which capital projects it wants to bond each year. In these cases, I would always start off by thanking the resident for their call and would apologize on behalf of the township. I would then explain the process in order that they would understand that it was not something I could simply order on my own. However, I always wanted to be able to offer something to them. That is the idea of good government. We are here to serve, so I made sure that was exactly what I did every time. I believe that the only thing most residents want is to be treated with respect and have someone listen to them. Therefore, if I was not able to pave a street just yet, I would ask them things such as, "Is there a tree of yours which needs trimming?" or "Do any of your sidewalks need repair, or perhaps potholes in your street?" These actions demonstrated that I was serious about my intention to help them. Rather than they hang up feeling frustrated about the larger issue which may need time and capital to address, they hung up having received something. As a result, they were happy taxpayers experiencing good government serving them when needed.

- *The public can be forgiving. But you must get out ahead of something. It is never the original mistake which leads to the* demise of a political career. It's the cover-up; the failure to tell the truth.

- You will find that most of the public are actually wonderfully nice people. That's why you will never interact with 95% of them. You will wind up interacting with a small group of people. Make every attempt to engage with members of the public and seek opportunities to allow for them to experience the work of a true public servant.

- Learn to see things the way others see things. Talk to people every day, Try to think the way people around you think; your subordinates, staff, etc. Learn how to hold and see two opposing viewpoints at the same time. This will assist in decision making as well as working out concessions with others.

- See the best in people for, if not, this business will send you crazy!

- When dealing with members of the press, always be mindful of their deadlines. Work at establishing a good rapport. Remember, their job is to report on a story. You can help craft the message behind a story by giving them as much background and information as possible. I had nothing but wonderful experiences with the press. Do the right thing and you have nothing to fear. They have a job to do and so do you.

CONCLUSION

If you have the calling, politics is a purposeful and fulfilling experience. By being a part of the solution rather than the problem, you play your part as a spoke on the larger wheel of politics which, in the final analysis, is the business of how society works.

This book has put forth a great amount of information for your review. While it is written from the perspective of my experiences, I believe that what I shared is universal and can apply to a multitude of situations. Also, not everything is for everyone. My style may not be compatible with yours. That's fine. That's the way it should be. However, despite your own style there is one thing on which I insist. Recognize the role you play, the position you hold and stay true to yourself and your oath. Do the right thing, always!

In addition to the outward appearances you develop and the skills you use, make every attempt to learn about government, law and the latest regulations. In New Jersey, we have an extensive amount of public service classes at Rutgers University in which you can enroll and even get certified. Things such as Land Use, tax and public policy, land development and redevelopment, etc., are all things with which you will be dealing in some form or another. Why not learn about them and come across as one who is well-versed in his or her position. There are many experts who share their expertise and most are happy to answer a question you may have if you call them. Frankly, the public, themselves, should demand their officials have studied and learned such things. By your proactively doing so, you are setting yourself apart and demonstrating true professionalism.

Only you have the power to make things happen. Stay humble, be kind, and stay true. That is my hope and my advice to all politicos. Good luck! Make us proud!

ABOUT THE AUTHOR

Brian Haggerty is a motivational speaker, author, educator and mentor. He is also the creator of the CLASS™ and PLEASE™ Programs. He is the author of the book, "Put That Cell Phone Down and Look Me in the Eye: Developing Masterful People Skills for Success at Any Age." To learn more, you may visit his web site BrianHaggerty.com. Brian served two terms on the Board of Commissioners for the Township of Lyndhurst. He also held various positions in political parties, has served on various public and political boards and has been as a public speaking and image coach to politicians and executives. He comes from a lengthy, full line of family involvement in politics since the 19th century.

Made in the USA
Columbia, SC
03 December 2018